Interactive Press

Things That Get You

Andrew Hubbard was born and raised in a small fishing village on the coast of Maine. He graduated from Dartmouth College magna cum laude, receiving awards in creative writing and psychology, and a degree in English. He completed his formal education at Columbia University, receiving a Master of Fine Arts degree in Creative Writing, summa cum laude. For most of his career, he worked as the Director of Training for a number of major financial institutions. He is a well-known speaker on the topic of corporate training, and has authored three books and dozens of articles on the subject. He is a former martial artist and competitive weight-lifter, a casual student of cooking and wine, a gemologist, a collector of edged weapons, a licensed handgun instructor, and an avid outdoor photographer. He currently lives in rural Indiana with his wife, two Siberian Huskies, and a demon cat.

Thanks for your support and enjoy the book !

Andy Hubbard

Interactive Press
The Literature Series

This book is dedicated to my children: Kurt, Andrew, and Lorelei. I only wish I could have taught you as much as you have taught me.

Things That Get You

Andrew S. Hubbard

"…Poetry and Hums aren't things which you get, they're things which get you."

– Winnie the Pooh

Interactive Press
an imprint of IP (Interactive Publications Pty Ltd)
Treetop Studio • 9 Kuhler Court
Carindale, Queensland, Australia 4152
sales@ipoz.biz
ipoz.biz/IP/IP.htm

First published by IP in 2014
© Andrew Hubbard, 2014

Printed in 12 pt Cochin on 14 pt Century Gothic.

National Library of Australia Cataloguing-in-Publication entry

Author:	Hubbard, Andrew S., author.
Title:	Things that get you / Andrew Hubbard
ISBN:	9781922120809 (paperback)
Subjects:	American Poetry
Dewey Number:	811.6

Contents

The Squirrel Who Loved Wind Chimes

"This is a little hard to believe…"

Nonetheless, the metal chimes hung from an eave
Outside the sliding glass door of the patio
And when the vagrant Wyoming wind
Pulsed through with energy to ring them
The squirrel came to participate.

"How do you know it was because of the chimes?"

Because when the chimes didn't ring
The squirrel didn't come.

"How do you know it was the same squirrel?"

Because he had a white fur scar on his left cheek.

"What did he do?"

He'd watch the chimes with the tail of his eye from the
patio railing,
Or sit beneath them with his paws crossed, looking up,
But his favorite trick was to cling to the roof edge
Right above the chimes, and hang down staring at them
With his tail twitching, then run across the roof with a
scratching clatter,
Then back to do it again.

Once he left an offering: three acorns
Nosed together, right beneath the chimes.

"Why, do you think?"

I don't know.

I wish I'd seen him do it.

"No, I mean why did he like the wind chimes?"

I've thought about it.
I don't know.
I think maybe he was a Newton, a Mozart of squirrels
And he heard more than other squirrels,
More than we do.

"And then what happened?"

He stopped coming.
Maybe a hawk had something to do with it.
Maybe not.

But after an interval
I honored him
By taking down the chimes.

Voices Behind The Waterfall

(Cumberland Falls, Kentucky)

Falling leaves
Falling water
Incautious kids (too near the edge)
Anxious mommy ("be careful")
Wise dog bemused
Not quite getting the point of the venture
But enjoying it thoroughly nonetheless

Stately bridge in sight upstream
A theme of arches repeated
And dark stains shaped like tears
But tears I think of contentment

And the bright, swift, combing water
Now clear, now gray, riffed with foam
Shoots into space, finds a new purpose:
To drop and create a voice —
A primal, low pitched roar
On a note that never seems to vary.

Behind the roar
I seem to sense voices
At the very edge of hearing
Almost comprehensible
Drifting away when I concentrate
Intruding when I'm unaware
Becoming clearer until I focus
Then fading again.

In these proud mountains of Kentucky
You could think spirits,
Indians with a closer kinship
To time and place.

Or you could say it's just our damned mind
With its insistence
On imposing order on chaos
Trying to find words in plain noise
(Same as we saw Jesus
And a triceratops
In some sunny afternoon clouds.)

But I don't believe either one.
I think something whispers to us
Now and then
In circumstances that seem random to us

With a message
That might give understanding
Or comfort or even wisdom
If we had the concentration,
Or the will, or the simplicity
To listen correctly.

But we don't,
At least I never have.

But the sense is always there
Growing and then fading
Like the voices behind the waterfall.

Yes, something whispers to us
But I don't know what.

The Boatshell

White and red,
Thumb-sized
And shaped something
Like a boat
To a little boy's fervent imagination

At water's edge
At cove's north side
I placed you down
So many times
With breathless lips
And tremulous fingers
To see if you would
Sink or swim.

And it was a game
Of fair deliverance
For a little boy:

Because sometimes you went down
On the first wavelet
Davy Jones'd in half a foot
Of cold harbor water
Ready for me to fish you out
And launch again.

And sometimes you bobbed away
Slowly on a windrift
Or current-pull, seeming
Glad
And free.

And I was glad
For you, with you,
As with any enterprise

Where the outcome is uncertain
But if attained by some flurry
Of luck, and wind, and perseverance
A cause for simple gladness at the core.

And our boatshell
(Not just mine any more)
Bobs and ducks
In the seabreeze and sundazzle.

Hood Ornaments

(Kimbal, Nebraska)

There are few things
More important to me
Than the line of three, long-abandoned cars
That I photographed near noon
In a huge, golden, rolling field
In colossal heat
In light so pure it hurt
In ringing High Plains silence.

Leaning together
Stripped of every useful thing
Down to their essence
One hood ajar in a shadow grin
One windshield out
One exhausted door hanging open.

They meant something,
They meant much
But it's impossible to say just what.

I worked the scene with a camera
And with whirling appreciation
For the thing itself.

Music From Stones

Stones can sing
And at certain times
Under certain circumstances
To certain people
They do.

If you love,
Or more, if you entertain
Memories of love,

Love that emphatically was
Or even love that could have been
But was checkmated
By rude fate

Then listen correctly
And these stones

[These: they ring a pool
Where the almost full moon floats
And a little girl
Practices magic words
With a patient father
Always humble
Always feeling
His children give him
More than he could possibly return]

These, I said,
Will sing to you
Of things stones know

Of durability against time,
Obdurate selfness,
Sensitivity to cold, to heat,
To things stones care about:

Arrangement, respect
Being of quiet service:
Singing a song so few can hear

And even those who hear
Unknowing of their hearing
Only saying to the little girl
"Let's sit here. Here on the rocks,
I think I hear the moon."

What The Rabbit Taught

I feel a linkage to the high plains...
The bluffs, the proud history of Indians and Plainsmen
The vast sweep of empty space
Deer, owls, and operatic coyotes,
Mile-long trains loaded with coal.

Wind was a constant theme,
Drawing through the scrub pines
On the ridge above us, and in the ravine
Below, where the wild turkeys had a home.

We had searing cold, pounding heat
And squid-ink black clouds piling in
From the west, bearing rain gushers
Or hailstones, once so big they killed a neighbor's horse.

After that storm our roof was a field of dents,
And two days later I traced a smell
Under some bushes and found two rabbits
Rotting, attended by flies
Hips broken, skulls crushed, legs askew.

My first thought was of Vesuvius
And the poignant tales those people tell us
Of love and terror...
But they at least had some conception
Of what was going on.

What would be on a rabbit's mind
When the beneficent sky
Provider of sun and rain and wind
Throws frozen, random bolts
That maim and agonize and kill?

What rabbit cosmology
Could make it make sense?

Even if the event
Proved cosmology wrong
I think the rabbits
Would require the teaching
To bear the circumstance.

But it's probably a mistake
To weigh down two dead rabbits
With a load of metaphysics.

I put on heavy gloves
Bagged the rabbits with clenched teeth,
And washed my hands for a long time.

First Impressions

(Brazos Bend State Park, Texas)

Almost another world
To a dour Down-Easter
Raised on the notion
That summer's
An interval between blizzards.

The first things you see
Are signs telling you
How not to be
Alligator lunch.

And then quietness
Space, and the place
Begins to pull you in.

Stillness.
Immensity of heat.

Huge, majestic trees
With spumes and streamers
Of Spanish Moss. "They look
Like souls," my daughter said.

I shouldn't mind my soul
To be so held by a strong branch
Hung out to sense
The sweetly humid air
Exotic bird calls, rain,
Moonrise over canebrake.

Beach Walk

Who would have thought
All those years ago
That we would have endured
Past all those couples
Brighter, richer, self-assured
So into themselves
And the game.

Decade has layered
Over decade.

Our children almost grown.
They think they're grown
Of course.

Not trophy kids, but ours
Straight and strong and loving
Banging their heads against the world
Just like we did.

We walk a deserted autumn beach
On Galvaston Island.

Heavy winds,
Great blocked clouds
Tumbling over the uneasy sea.

The proud supertankers
Lumber into port.
Surprisingly, they don't seem
Out of place.

We scooch down
To really appreciate
The tracks of whelks,
Hermit crabs, bubbling clam holes.

The long stone jetties
Hold fishermen with morning beers
Cigarettes, minnows.

One suspicious pelican
With half-spread wings.

The sun breaks through
And for a moment
Illumination tickles
The darting shore birds into flight.

We don't say much —
Savoring the burnished rush
Of wind, of sand,
Of years.

Rain On A Muddy Trail

Cold, cold December rain
And a deer standing quizzical
In the path ahead, one hoof lifted
Motionless, tail raised in alarm
Deeply untrusting, but curious still.

Ears wag; seem to say:

"What is this man-thing
Alone, so far from his kind
On a shiver-wet morning
At the beginning of the time
When it's hard to find food?"

He snorts a ghost of breath,
Stamps a forefoot, pretends not to care,
Ambles a step or two,
Turns sedately off the path,
Disappears, and then I hear him
Crash away through sodden bracken
As though my demons
Might change their focus
And fishhook themselves
Onto his gentle soul.

He leaves silence, rain,
Hoofprints beautiful as etchings
And his guileless question:

What is this man-thing
Alone, so far from his kind?

Old Post

Leaning from the wind
Like an old scarecrow
This fence post —
Last one standing
In a field no more a field,
On a farm no more a farm —
Pokes his ragged gray self
To the first streak of sun.

The tangled growth around him
Dips to the stroke of sunrise
And like a miracle,
A bluest morning glory
Has chosen this post,
To wrap itself around
And lift its trumpet mouth
To tell us what it knows
About unselfconscious energy,
The will, the becoming.

House Sitting In Brattleboro

Sojourners for a season
In an old farmhouse
Dour and bleak
As this cold, wet Vermont spring

I stand in the old, cold pantry
Once home to bags of potatoes
Barrels of cider, molasses and cured pork

Now crammed with dry cereal,
Diet soda, pop tarts,
Chip bags the size of pillows.

I am skulking:
Avoiding floorboards that creak
Moving like a cat burglar
Hiding from my wife
Who would kill me for my own good
If she caught me in my sin.

I am having a meal
Of canned peaches
      (from the can)
And apricot brandy
      (from the bottle).

Part of me laughing at myself:
The paucity of my transgressions
And the loving see saw
Of marital politics.

Part of me transported,
Utterly beguiled and consumed
By my baser appetites.

I do a reality check
With my soul for guilt
And find none.

That's a relief.

After all, what philosopher
Has found a coda as compelling
As sugar and alcohol
On the sly, in a darkening pantry
Looking out through windows
So old the glass has warped
At the last bold light, framing
A deer beneath the old apple tree.

Mammoths

I almost bought
A fossil mammoth tooth
For three hundred dollars.
But it could have been fake
(I wouldn't know!)
And as I pointed out to myself
It's not a thing you really need.

Still, I love those great brutes
So perfectly evolved for a world
Not they nor our own resilient forbears
Could imagine ever changing.

I wonder, have any of us
Now alive seen a thing so majestic
As their crossed tusks tossing at the sky,
Their measured footfalls across a snowy plain.

Maybe not. Size does
In some elemental way
Confer dignity and worth.

I'd like to think
Some beneficent cosmic mastermind
Has provided these beings
A home—a spirit home—
Of blowing snowfields
Rich moss and tundra grass
Dim, dim sun
And kin to make the journey
Real and safe and cold.

Richard's Squirrel

A car-struck squirrel
With blood at his nose
And worthless hips
Crawls most slowly
With blazing pain
All about him
Toward the grass
Toward the maple trees
Where he so recently
Was such the proud
And cocksure acrobat.

Now no more
And never again to be.

Such a turn of fate
In such a reckless instant.

My heart went out to him.
Felt him say
Like all the pained, bewildered creatures
"Daddy, make the hurt stop."

And I couldn't,
So I watched him recede
In my rearview mirror
Almost running off the road
And down a sheer embankment.

Almost sharing his fate
Almost fractured beyond mending
Almost a bloody mess in shattered metal.

My hands shook on the steering wheel
And I knew soul compassion
For the squirrel, my brother.

Placement

When first I come back
Into these deep woods
Dark with mid-day shadow
Thick with memories
Now a generation old

I feel very much
A jarring intruder
Out of place, mistimed,
Unwelcome.

And then I slow myself.
With deliberation
Sit or walk
Among the dignity
Of this place
And slowly become
Re-accepted.

I am at home here
And I know
Beyond words
The meaning of home.

November Scripture

The preacherman
Looks for inspiration
At the bullet-headed hawk
Cruising by, hunting,
Assured in his ferocity
His untroubled certainty
That the world is for hawks.

Their food a birthright,
Their enemies a tribulation bestowed by god
(A hawk of great wisdom)
To test their worth and courage.

Preacherman: what do you see?
Is the vision one of perspective,
One of humility?

Does watching a hawk hunt
Make you wish for wings
And a hawk's certitude
Of its place at the apex of creation?

We know, we think we know,
That faith should be strong
And doubt is weakness.

By this measure
The hawk wins, clearly:
Preacher is nothing if not doubt,
Conflict, ambiguity, and irresolution.

The hawk sits at the end
Of an outreaching oak branch

Bobs his head, fans his tail feathers
And stares a silent moment

At the preacher, hunching his shoulders
To the spitting rain
Distancing across a long field
Laden with tumbled autumn clouds
And a gaggle of crisp leaves spinning overhead.

Back home in his dark study
The preacher has a sermon to get done.

He takes another pill
For the headache that never quite goes away,
Pours sherry into a coffee mug
Adjusts the light, drums his pen
Reflects, deems the hawk
A metaphor too abstruse
For his small and inattentive congregation.

A Momentary Stay

Limned by starlight only
There is a black apple tree
Old and still, in a field
Gone to seed, on a hillside
Fallow, once worked, now no more.

Late spring, the night hot,
A few blossoms cling
But most have gone.

There is silence,
And the stillness is great
Save once when an owl coasts by
Blackening a moving swath of stars.

Those tremulous light points
That seem to have so much
To say, yet in the end
Speak more to science than to art.

Still, they make for me
At least a point of reference
And I derive serenity
From that relationship
Tenuous as it may be.

It's quite enough
For me, for now,
To have a place.
My own coordinates.

(Haphazard,
But I like it that way.)

In sight of many stars
Near an apple tree
In a field, along a hill

In a dispensation
Of abundant time,
Season of tranquility.

The Old Hay Loft

The hay in the barn
(The barn long abandoned)
Darkens from straw to brass to gold
And wilts most slowly in upon itself.

In summer it heats
From internal compacted moisture
Until almost it burns.
In winter it grows
Crackles of feathery frost,
Most beautiful —
Ecstasy for a geometer.

But most of all it endures,
In a barn with bowed beams
Doors looted by neighbors
Holes in the roof
And paper wasp palaces
Stuck to the inner roof.

It endures with a will
That does not even have a name
Or a purpose it can call its own.

It endures because endurance
Is what it knows, and all it knows.

Sidewinder At Noon

A cold snake
On hot sand
With death in its jaws

Weaving a waved track
On sand that sparkles
In the brutal sun.

Disturbed, you must have been
To be out now

When even your thick skin
And stilleto fangs
Ache with the awful heat

What disturbs you?
What foreboding fills you with unease?

Good questions are difficult,
Answers are harder still.

And they will come
Not from you
Winding your way
Into a clump of succulents and weeds

And not from this place
Disjointed but for heat
That burns clear through me.

Questions shall be answered, if at all
By grace itself
If grace should touch me:

27

Back-pedalling
(Ungainly, but fast as I can go)
In primordial fear

From a sidewinder
Undulating
Then disappearing
In this ferocity of heat.

Toward Hog Island

I think to myself:
"There is nothing as rhythmic
As rowing a skiff
Across a long expanse
Of calm water."

The bow slaps the water
After each pull,
The oarlocks do a two part
Squeak and creak
As I stroke and recover,
And the oars bite
And release the water
With a crisp splash going in;
A foamy rush coming out.

This set against the sound
Of my hard breathing
And the half heard thud
Of blood in my head and neck.

Such a compilation of beats —
Who could sort it out?
And why try? It works together
To engender reflection

Reflection becomes a doorway
To contemplation, and this afternoon
Of contemplation in motion
Might have brought forth
Some burst of insight.

It didn't, but that seems not to matter.

It was – it is – the process
Of living for a while in contemplation
Unconscious of itself
That consecrates the time
And makes the work of rowing
Quiet pleasure.

Every now and then I pause.

Skiff and reflection drift,
And I lift my shirt
To wipe the sweat off my face.

I swivel in my seat to see
Behind me
The little island I am rowing toward.

I had seen it as a haven
(Much needed)
But on the way I found
The journey was the destination;
The island only needed for perspective.

Truth And Relativity

I had not thought or wished
To live beyond the life
Of beliefs I was raised in.

(We know, reluctantly,
That values and beliefs
And truths themselves
Have a lifespan,
And at the end expire
Just as surely
As if they were flesh.)

Before I was tall enough
To see the countertop
My mother taught me
The lore of crows.

"Birds are more than birds,"
She would say, and teach me:

"One crow sorrow, two crow joy
Three crow letter, four crow boy
Five crow silver, six crow gold."

And when I saw five crows
Flapping silently on a still sky
And later my father gave me a silver dime
I knew that it was true.

Dying Gods

A young Greek girl
Whoring for her god in the temple
Brought down that temple
And with it, in her long-forgotten dust
An array of such gods as shall not be seen again.

Who would have thought
Such little, vile acts
Could have such repercussion?

And what, I wonder,
Do dying gods think about?

That's a question I do believe
We shall never ever answer,
But it nags, nonetheless.

When immortality,
So long taken for granted
That it seems neither privilege nor curse,
Is found to be temporary
The adjustment must be… difficult,
An extraordinary fracture
Of the universal harmony.

I think if it were me,
Once I grasped that it was ending,
I would crave annihilation
Out of rage and shame
And feelings we are not given to know.

I would not think a god
Could forswear dignity and station

For some brutish existence
In a ravaged realm, bereft
Of equals, of passion, of intrigue,
Scorned by those who used to worship.

Better oblivion.
Better not to look back on grandeur
Or ahead to days like ours
With reverence in senescence
Imagination in such poverty
It speaks in halting whispers
And scarce can find a home.

Dreamwalker

Fruit of desperation
Fruit of resignation
In troubled sleep
I am holding a clifface
With screaming shoulders
A tangle of unforgiving rocks far below.

A toss of ragged wind
A stutter of cold rain
No hope whatsoever
Of getting out alive.

I shudder awake
With pillow soaked
Thigh muscles jumping
Afraid to go back to sleep
For fear the dream will replay
As it sometimes does.

In the morning I get up
And don't think much about it.
Just one of those things.

Some people have allergies or migraines
I have these dreams.

The thing to do
Is to do the things
That must be done.

I have a job to go to,
Bills to pay (God knows!)
And the kids start school next week

So the days go.
Not too bad after all.
It's the nights.

So I stall in the bathroom
Have a last martini
And finally lie down
Knowing what darkness brings.

Mcdonald's Man

There are a lot more street people
Than ten years ago.

And this one, in McDonald's,
Where we went after the play
For my wife to get tea
Struck me for two reasons.

He said, "Thank you ma'am"
When he got his coffee, and said it
With the nuance we call cultivation.

And he put his change
In the lucite donation box
Beside the cash register.
Odd: he must have begged hard
And swallowed much pride
For those two wrinkled dollars.

"He should have gotten protein;
He needs protein,"
I muttered to my wife.
"Why coffee?"

..."It's cold. He's cold," she replied.

The line moved ahead.
We got her drink.

The guy sat hunched
Under bright lights
With a ten day peppered beard
And wisps of white hair askew
Moving his lips
Avoiding looks
Effacing himself.

Gripping the coffee with two shaking hands
(Delicate fingers, but dirty,
And yellow, corrugated nails.)

We were heading out
I hesitated, took my wife's arm:

"I want to buy him a sandwich,
But I don't know how to ask him.
If he doesn't want it
He'll be insulted.
But he doesn't look good.
I don't know what to do."

… "Just go."

I teased: "Usually you're the softie."

…"He scares me."

"How can a 60 year old guy with nothing
But a green, plastic, carry-bag
Scare you?"

… "He just does. Let's go."

"He's just sitting there.
You can't live on coffee."

… "I don't care. Let's go."

We went. Her feet
Rapped in anger against the asphalt.

And I know her well enough
To know she doesn't know
If the anger is for me
Or her, or just the situation.

Battle Scars

When your hard breath
Against cold glass
Turns window into mirror
Then you see
What you'd rather not:

Vertical seams
In a face you thought you knew
A face you grew into
Through the years,
A face you regretfully admit
You deserve.

At your age my friend,
A face seldom lies.
It has lost both will and ability
To dissemble
Successfully
For very long.

You can try it out
In dim bar light
When the whisky trance
Makes you think
You look like you think
You used to think you looked like.

But that doesn't work
Very much, very well, very long.

And then you're stuck
With the hard bounce back

To a reality unforgiving
And uninterested in your vanity.

Better to suck it up,
Get on with it,
Make your peace
With the time-bitten face
The screaming knees and flaring back
The way the young girls
Look right through you
Because to them
You're not really there.

Wishbone Impossible

So much excitement
It was hard to breathe!

Wishbone
Heartbone
Proud Mommy
Helps us giggling kids
To twine little fingers
Round the wishbone's dried legs
And pull! --Who gets
The centerpiece gets his wish.

Those wishes!
So humble, so unselfconscious,
So delicate in the web of simplicity
That circumscribed our lives
In those tumble-backed years.

It's not nostalgia
Or vapid sentimentality
That makes these memories
Hard to hold
Impossible to release.

It's the knowledge
Of times gone irrevocably
Places changed unrecognizably
Values lost, dreams defiled
Memories of love and wonder
Impossible to appreciate at the time
And now impossible to recapture
Impossible to outlive.

A Contender

What do you do with dreams
That won't come true
In spite of resolute execution
Sincerity and perseverence?

None die with a bang
Some with a whimper
But more retreat
To rationalization,
To things we rarely speak of.

And when they come up
It's with a facile cover story
A spin that makes it ok
Or inconsequential.

A throwaway line
Tagged to a martini
And a mouth full of shrimp and bacon.

"I was gonna play football
But my knees...."

"I had a recording contract
But I wouldn't do it their way...."

"I had this idea
But my partner stole it...."

Those dreams,
Like once-plump
Helium balloons
A week past prime

Furrowed and wilted
And hanging by a string
Just above the floor.

Does it take more courage
To keep an improbable dream flickering
Or give it up and call it failure?

Heavy Wind

There's nothing I love as much
As heavy wind.

Nature's irregular heartbeat
Coming on strong
Only now and then
To send leaves
Scuttering down the street
Or coiling them up in deep pockets
Near our door, and at the fence corner.

The Mexican Fans
With their stiff hands
Clash hard against the house
And high palms lean with the wind:

As I cannot
Who love the wind so much
I must leave for a wooded park
Where I can walk face upturned
To watch where wind bites
And saws through treetops

Bowing them down
Through — not anger — just energy
That primal push to be
To exercise existence
Against those things
That might dare to hold it back.

But I can't do that
I have more restraint
Have learned consideration
Tact, and the other person's point of view.

A shame.

I'd rather see myself
Howling through trees and adversity
With a flat roar
Even if that should mean
Dying out at last in some wasted place
Played out, worn,
Bereft of energy
But by God saying,
"I blew down a few trees
Along the way
And did the thing
As it should be done."

A Wendy Day

The wind-riled chop
Beat back against our skiff,
Pushed us homeward
Back off the little island
Where we'd thought to picnic
Thought to wander among the pine and spruce
On the little island called Clam-Hod
Uninhabited (so far as we know)
By any but pine and spruce
Oh, of course sea-grass, millet sedge
And the small flowers: purple, white, and pink
Without names, but of such delicate beauty
You part the grass around them
To give them extra sun
But never ever touch them.

About the wind —
Offshore and heavy-handed
It didn't want us to go there that day.

And heeding fate
We turned southwest
To a little cove
We like to think
We alone had found.

And there the wind symphony played high above us
Our simple meal a sacrament,
And there you came to be.

And Windy would have been so odd a name
That everyone would get it wrong
From school to passport to driver's license.

So we succumbed to Wendy,
And now you know.

A Death In The Family

We saw, ruefully,
How death brought out the worst
In most we knew.

When this one died
Or that one, almost
Before the last breath rattled out

The children and the siblings
The creditors and the ex's

Showed up with backs arched
Like Cats of Kilkenny
To scrabble and scheme
With disproportionate passion
For bits of money and junk
So paltry not even lawyers
Had an interest.

And those who got the loser's share
Were so aggrieved
They left sincerely vowing
Retribution and eternal hatred.

So families are sundered:
Over costume jewelry
Plywood end tables
And cars that won't even start.

Folly, greed,
Envy, and spite
Played out on a field
So circumscribed
That self-respecting mice
Would be ashamed.

Two Crows

Two crows
Near the top
Of a dead tree
(Leafless — a collection
Of pipestem scrawl branches
Against an after-sunset sky).

Not looking at each other
But so intensely aware
Each of the other
That they are bonded

Though it's hard to say just how.

One preens,
Nibbles under a wing
Flexes foot across foot
Down the windstripped branch.

Other looks off unmoving
Past sunset, past owlcall
A contemplative
Of crow world.

So same
So alien
Me to them
And them to me.

The same path
Trees, gravel, roiled cloudsong
Riven moon afloat now
Still pale against the sun's

Feeble remnants, but with promise
Of bold luminescence
A real stay against the terrible darkness.

The crows and I
We see the same thing yet they see nothing I see
And I deeply suspect
I see nothing that they see.

Crow world:
Balanced, harmonious
Inscrutable to us lower forms
Crunching on the gravel path
Below, earthbound
Passing in deepening twilight
Passing in
One hopes
Mutual respect.

Turnabout

The first cable
Was from your body to theirs
Indisputable, conveying
Life by the moment,
Shucked off at birth
So weirdly strange to see it go.

The second cable
Was crying need.
The predictable bellow
For attention, food, play,
The necessary wipedown.
A tether ranged
From blatant helplessness
To glum / loving responsibility.

And then the dissolving cable
Of tweens, adolescents, twisters,
Needing us less and ever less.

The table turning slowly
Like an old railroad roundhouse
But relentless, spurred
By guilt and obligation
And cold, cold money.

Oh, and love too
Real enough in hindsight
But easy to lose
In the daily clatter of events.

"Your Mom needs her prescription."
"Dad can't lift that any more."

And worse to come, for sure
As the gates of youth
Slam shut against us
One after another
After another after another.

Leaving us – how delicately fortunate –
Still in love, but less abled,
Dazed and gently confused
By the overwhelming rush of things.

Casting a finespun cable back
To you kids, a lifeline
Back... a cable...
Now it's your turn.

Trolling Off Northport

Some fall days are warm enough
Others: not really

This — one of the latter.

We run the sloop under power
(A thing he never liked)
At 2, 3 knots, no more
And set a course
Toward the raking,
Hard-bitten North Atlantic
Where the real fishermen
Haul Turbot, Hake, and Halibut
From the cornucopious Grand Banks.

We're not them
But respect the craft.

We drop our lines
Watch them where air and water meet
Draw a line like the finger of time
Through the steel gray chop.

The wind picks up
Decks the waves with a frieze of foam.

We raise wool collars
Drink a little dark rum
From a square-faced bottle in the sternsheets.

Later, with the wind
Down to cat's paws
We moor in an inlet of reeds

With blocked clouds tackling heaven
And one bright, orange lance
Of sunset light shining through.

We caught nothing
But ventured much.

And not long later
In the hot, hot south
In the burnished hum
Of a hospital elevator
As you went down
You said, "I think I'm really sick."

You were, of course, right.

Did we foreshadow anything?
Learn anything — one from another?

And have you found
The fisher of men?
Or was he us
And we let it go by

Or more likely
Caught it without knowing

In the deed itself:
The most noble and melancholy calling
Of casting out
And waiting
And hoping.

The Space Between Beats

The too-big grandfather clock
In the too-big room
Of the too-big house
Wheezes itself up to another hour.

Begins to strike
Its measured sonorous notes
For eleven post meridian.
The day almost done its particulars.

The notes strike a chord
But more eloquent
Is the ringing silence
Between each stroke.

A threat unspoken
But more foreboding for that
Of longer silence
Threading out
To a great destitution
Of time:
None left for us.

How did it happen?
Where did it go –
Was it in the grocery bags,
The parent-teacher conferences
The Halloween dress-ups
The endless loads of laundry and dishes?

Maybe it was the birthday parties
The unfinished photo albums
The leash-tugged, late night dog walks

Shopping lists, Christmas lists
Death march procession of bills.

Dirty coffee cups
Empty beer cans
Haircuts, dentist appointments
Check registers shoved in drawers
So jammed they never shut right.

The first appalling gray hairs,
The pains you instantly hope
Are just a momentary mistake.

The faint lines
Then not so faint:
A roadmap to a reckoning
Of strange duality...
Inevitable but incomprehensible
Foreknown yet inconceivable.

The Speed Of Dark

(Nightfall on the Allegheny River, Pittsburgh, PA)

The river is alive tonight.
Across the water, city lights
Cut the night
Shimmer in broken patterns
On the river surface.

In the black and silver arabesque
I see history.

The vital forest
Known only to itself

And then the small persistent interlopers:
First Nation, Iroquois,
Voyageur, Pole, Croat,
Factory builder, steel worker
Smokestack flecks in their lungs
Tough hands, sore eyes,
Ingrown pain in the lower back.

The unthinkable in the 70's:
Mills closing, razed for parking lots.

Men sit on sagging stoops
Of the tipsy houses
On the heart-attack hills
With Iron City Beer
Wondering what happened –
Whatever happened?

The dark river slides west to the Mississippi
Cold, deep, unconcerned.

A pair of geese fly low and fast
Across the river in the new dark
Certain of their destination.

The moon breaks out
Above the eastern ridge
And shows a family of five rabbits
Amazing, tenacious little knots of fur
All nuzzled into grass.

Too close to the road!

I herd them back toward the river
Toward safety, toward darkness.

The 16ᵗʰ Street Bridge Song

Who would have thought
This utilitarian bridge

With its too narrow lanes
And uninspired graffiti

This humpbacked trestle
With big inch bolts by the thousand
And garish yellow paint

Could sing?

Who'd've thought
This aging urban eyesore
With soot-caked, faux medieval corner stations,
Where I walk at sunrise
With a pain in my hips like fire
And a fire in my heart like pain

Could sing?

Who would have thought
That this monument to tastelessness
With its elevated, skeletal, copper balls
Filled with horses symbolizing… something
Would honor me with transport
From the thing I call home
To the thing I call work.

And sing.

It has a dignity that overwhelms design.

It has confident purpose.

And as I walk across its strength
In the morning, with my shadow stretched behind me
And in the evening, with my shadow stretched behind me,
It sings to me

Of the strength of flowing rivers,
Of the need for rivers

Of the steadfastness of bridges,
Of the need for bridges.

Slanted Headstone

We marked a slanted headstone
On a west-facing hillside
In a country graveyard
Off a road still not tarred
In a town unincorporated
Off the beaten path
Of this young and turbulent century.

Scarce tended by the man
With a charitable sincecure
To mow and trim the county cemeteries.

(Charitable: son of an alderman
Himself a bank director
Now a saddened, sodden sot
Buying booze for underage kids
And getting from the deal
A daily bottle for himself.)

Back to the headstone

Soft gray rock, cheap,
(Not the good local granite)
And worked with a hand
Of the times, peculiar
Archaic A's and G's
Put down in this stony
Unrelenting earth
To tell us a story
Stark, without detail
Or texture or commentary
Of a man who was born
And then, somewhat later, died.

We struggle to make out
The name and dates:
26? 31? Knowles? Notting?
It's unclear.

And the stone
With high regard for frost
Tilts obliquely westward
Toward the chill sunset
And the mountains of New Hampshire.

We Were Boys

We were boys
And we found once in the woods
A headstone-shaped slice of granite,
Man-sized, the only rock around.
It lay on its back in a bed of moss and lichen
In a dense wood of evergreen and birch.

Gold and blue-green
The lichen veiled its surface
Yet it seemed to us its roughness
Was chiseled with lines and suns
And things that could be fish or sails.

We were boys
We stood on the rock
Scraped at the lichen with our soles,
Ran fingers over the abraded surface,
And went on to other things.

The earth and moon danced on
A score of years.

Now I couldn't find the place.

Now I doubt and wonder
If rain and sun and frost
Had roughened the stone
And the rest was all imagination.

Or maybe not,
Maybe that hard tongue
Had much to tell
Of those who came before:
Their triumphs and their trials.

Evidence and probability
Suggest frost;
Romance and wishful thinking
Go another way –
Suggest far warriors
Pridefully chiseling their deeds
Into hard, hard stone.

Heroes. They were heroes.
And like heroes
They shared a little,
And left us mostly questions,
As heroes do.

Settlement

A split moon
Hovers above this house
Of small dramas —

A career in jeopardy
Boys flown
A girl in adolescence:
All confusion and excitement
Clothes and friends and clothes
And things she — of course —
Duh! Can't tell us.

And for us the light touch
Of age… soon to bear down hard!

Hair color, vanishing cream,
Recalcitrant fat
Dental bills the size of elephants
Regiments of orange plastic pill bottles
Containing we-can't-remember-what
But-just-take-it-anyway.

Still there are rewards, achievements,
Things to savor: the draped wisteria fringe
A-hum with bees;
A gigantic black cat
Friendly as a brick
Sprawled across my work desk
Green eyes turned inward
On a vision of self-satisfaction.

And the quiet tick
Of your sleep breathing
As I lie awake
And watch the violet scribble
Of heat lightning
And sense the squeeze and thump
Of my heartbeat
Still good, still good for a while.

Separation

The motels are as alike
As slices of white bread.
Strong locks, weak mattresses,
Art the visual equivalent of oatmeal,
And everything bolted down (as though
Any sane person would steal it.)

The patrons—now there's some interest!
A few tingling lovers (illicit, one hopes).
The families: Dads grim, Moms frazzled
Kids with Game Boys and Doritos
Mostly crying or sleeping
Or in transit between the two.
Grimly optimistic salesmen/women
With their unobjectionable clothes
And secret stash of scotch or weed.
And the faceless middle management functionoids
Doing their marketing or training or whatever
For Wichita, Syracuse, Jacksonville.

Them! I'm one of them!
On the cell each night
A broken wisp of digital connection
To the real life
The one I return to
Near sleep, and near waking.

Lorelei got a good report card,
Kurt didn't, Andy won't tell.
The dog threw up; the cat didn't come home.
The car's making a funny noise
And nobody can understand the cable bill.

How could anybody call this poignant?
And yet, from weeks and states away,
It is, and that's all there is to it.

I miss you,
Call me.
I'll call you tomorrow
After the meeting.

Rolling Dice

It won't do
It won't do
To overdo
That mystic stuff

But our most profound
Recalcitrant question
Always
From our early breaths of wonder
Is "why?"

Those early answers
"Because it is."
"Because Mommy says so."
Do for a while.

Then they don't
And we're on a quest
Not of our choosing
But thrust upon us
By... well...
That's the question, isn't it?

And it takes us,
Some of us – no –
All of us,
As far as we wish to go
On a path of our own making
Fresh to each
Unique to each
And yet the same
The same for every soul.

And we find what we find
In an organized spirituality
Or the soup of daily work
Or in the silent places.

And some perhaps go farther
With no effort,
Fated, graced somehow:
A nodding flower
Where the butterfly
Simply chooses to land
To slowly open its wings
Around the passionate light.

Outside The Bedroom Window

The Mexican Fan
With its rigid arcs
Of pleated green
Brushes vague fingers
Against our bedroom window

Tries to tell us something
In its hard fashion
Of bouncing raindrops off itself
Running stiff fingers
Against the glass in wind
Deflecting morning light
Through blinds onto us
Tousled, vagrant bed-slugs.

I wonder what it senses
Nodding, scratching
At the glass:
Nothing hostile I'm sure
No Poe raven
No horror movie "thing."

More probably
Gently contemptuous
Of us poor creatures who have to uproot
Move, work, and bluster
To achieve the same
Fulfillment he finds
In simple sunshine,
Simple rain.

Quick Pix

A hanging gull:
Birds have such a knack
Of taming wind
Fluting it to their purpose

And I see that bird
High up, motionless
In a strong wind

Feathers tipped exactly
To sustain
Its stay against confusion.

And I think the same –
The same thought I thought
When I saw that gull's
Great, great, great-grandfather
Do the same trick
In the same sky
Forty years ago:

Boy, I wish I could do that.

Eagle Creek Park

Some images seen once
Stay with you for a lifetime.

And I'm learning why.

The soul has totems
Unique to itself:
Colors, shapes, sounds
Degrees of light
Wind and stillness
Open space and seething crowds.

These things transmuting
Through layered time

I've waited ten years
To tell you I saw a wolf
Through a veil of falling snow
Close up! One forefoot raised,
Intent on me through the lens
Of his own perceptions, desires,
Faint, inherited memories.

His totems! I'd give a lot to know them,
But that's not in the cards.

I even had a camera
And was almost quick enough
To catch the encounter.

But then I wasn't fast enough,
And now I don't need it.

On Lying Awake At Night

Banshees of the city
Police sirens shriek
In the crouching dark

Approaching —
Then diminishing.

Later another
To the north I think,

Then a faint one
On the edge of hearing
(It might almost be a mosquito).

Then a pause,
Then one so close
My wife's sleep breathing
Breaks, hitches, resumes.

I watch black snakes
Moving against my eyelids
Hear the quiet clash
Of palms awash in wind
And the sleeping dog's long groan.

Mind flickers unbidden
From ever-throbbing knees
To incessant bills
The car's ominous rattle
The call I forgot to return.

Another siren – moving fast –
Hell bent on some young tough guy

With the energy for felony;
The courage or instinct
Never to reflect, only act
To defy sense, logic, and the odds

Feeding on the night
On danger – a short hot fuse
Quick to hate
To feel aggrieved.

Inarticulate
But not necessarily wrong for that.

I send him a good thought
Roll on my side
Will the snakes to be still.

Not A Good Morning

I stepped out of the house
And found our new cat's body
A tangled bloody mess
Splayed on the grass
One eye open, blank
One a clot of blood.

And knew of course at once
Our old cat, Kingston, had killed him.

My first thought:
How will I tell my wife
That the friendly one
The one who gave us head butts
In the middle of the night
Was just a smear upon the lawn.

My second thought:
We should have kept him in.
He just wasn't big enough yet
To fight for his life.

I retrieve the morning paper
From curbside, and Kingston
Comes running up to me, delighted,
Throws himself down on the springy grass
And rolls on his back
For a tummy rub
And then to be carried inside
For the scrambled egg treat
My wife is dishing up.

He eats crouched down
With his tail around his forepaws.

My Boys

Years ago they'd introduce me
To their teachers in voices brimming with pride:
"This is my <u>Dad</u>."
Now I grin to find myself just as proud saying:
"These are my <u>Boys</u>."

Late teens. So big. So entirely difficult.
So unswervingly certain to make every wrong decision.

Lazy, heedless, brains evidently on hold, except
Strange, unexpected flashes
Of the gentle, thoughtful kids they used to be.

Those give us hope.
"20 cures 16," I say
Because I want to believe it.

In the meantime
I surprise myself with patience,
Figure they'll grow up
<u>In spite</u> of me if not <u>because</u> of me
And smile to hear my hopeless clichés —
Get a job…
Do your homework…
Stop hitting your sister.

Back to the patience.

Partly I think it's resignation —
We've done what we can
By precept and example
To guide their character and values.
Now it's time to step back and watch

Proudly or ruefully
As they lurch through
Those so critical first grown up years.

And partly it's wistful sadness
Knowing how eager they are to leave
How well we know our role
To help them go and not look back.

This is the hardest thing:
Each year they need us less
And we need them more.

Lost Loves

Some seashells
Can be boats.
If set down gently enough
They will float – just barely
(If the water's calm
And the wind at rest.)

And if those circumstances
All are met
A boy with hopeful eyes
Can watch his shell
Dance bravely out
With what seems courage
And tranquility.

They never last very long.
A bigger wave
A cat's paw breeze
Or just the shell's
Own urge to sink
Will pull it down

Slip sliding through
The clear, cold salt water
To gain a toehold
On the bottom sand
And in anthropomorphic fashion
Retire from the fray.

The boy strains to see it
Through the surface gleams
Gives it up,

Launches another and another.

These beautiful, pearlescent
Bits of nature.
They never last very long.

Linkage And Rust

Nothing is so capricious
As memory. A jokester
Not kind, not sympathetic
Rebellious to even itselfr
Consistent in inconsistency
And implacable – that most of all.

Tonight it impels me back
To summer days of blueberry picking
Alone, around scrub spruce
Ledged granite, chipmunks, cloud shadows,
And – of all incongruities –
Hauled out there by someone
Years back, well forgotten
An old, small road-grader
Abandoned, with every useful part stripped off.

Degraded from usefulness
Flaking slowly in the summer sun
With a gift of golden rust
To the palm of a child who touched

Not a discarded artifact
But a wondrous thing
That seemed a master of time itself
In its forged, metallic decreptitude.

So different from the stolid spruces
That sighed appreciation

And the mica flecks
That winked off the shadow
Of a little boy
Intent on blueberries
And the unconscious necessity
Of driving a long, strange path
Whose purpose may only be
To provide an awkward
Ungainly inspiration
To my own little boys
And so on, further
In majestic generation.

A Love Cycle

One.

When your eyes kissed me
I saw our children
I saw our hands
Holding each other
Forty years from now.

Two.

Just eating french fries
You wiped the salt from your lips
With a careless finger
And I have never seen
Anything so erotic
In my entire life.

Three.

In sleep you are so vulnerable
I don't have the heart to wake you
I lie awake for hours
Waiting for you to stretch
And roll in my direction.

Four.

You rescued a baby rabbit
And cried when it died in your hand
And we knew together
The fragility of love and breath.

Five.

In this soft rain
In this quiet, wooded place
We walk together in gentle harmony
As close as people can be
And yet apart, for all of that.

North Park, November

Winter nibbles delicately
At the last shreds of fall

Sending shawling snow showers
Holy winter's Nuncio

Over these darkened
Passionate hills.

The first snowflakes
– Winter's baby teeth –
Pinwheel down with a soft hiss
On the crisp leaves
Still taut on the hard ground
Still holding a smoke of color
From their glory a month ago.

And I kneel on the forest floor
To hear, and to see
The leaf packs and root hollows
Slowly fill with snow.

Looking up, the snow is more determined now
Foaming around a million tree trunks.

It's hard to believe
That in their hundred years
These trees have not learned
A way to share experience
And feeling with their brethren.

Now a hard wind blast
Dervishes the snow
But barely rocks the trees
And perhaps they murmur:

"No matter. We've seen it before.
Spring will come."

And near me, one giant oak
Has caught the trunk
Of a fallen beech across a limb
And holds him far above the ground.

How might a tree feel
About a fallen brother...
And what centering might find us
In fresh snow on fallen leaves?

– for Scott Luster, after the death of his daughter

Grudgingly, Toward Prayer

Violets, Sunflowers, Roses.

Sunflowers with their two-day stubble
Of prickles on the stem.
Roses holding whispered glamour
Hints of hot, lascivious sin.
And violets like a yawning kitten's mouth.
(Eyes squeezed shut, tiny claws out.)

Something in perfection
Demands we question it:

We want the how and why,
We want a meaning.

The good scholars give us
500 million years of patient, ordered evolution

And we construct religion
To explain the things
We can't explain
And it serves, to a degree
But still we want proof that we will never have.

And so we dither
Like a squirrel crossing the road
And deciding
– Four times –
– In the middle –
That the other side is better.

Frankly, I don't ever see an answer
Unless a car comes along to settle the matter.

No Name Skiff

Among the long salt grass
A square-butted skiff sits
Waiting for a strong push
Into water, a heavy step,
A creak of oarlocks, scrape
Of shipping oars, then off
To who knows what adventures:
Water borne and salt sprayed
That never come to this lost skiff.

Owner died – moved away – or just
Moved on to other things.

And this skiff just left
Loveless but not forlorn
Hopeful in its quietness
With the paint slowly peeling
And the taut planks
Finally showing a little warp,
Nail heads slowly coming loose
The little craft subsiding
Sideways just a bit
In the long, uncaring grass
Just yards above the tide pull
Set to be safe
And safe enough surely
But aching for usefulness
To feel the thud of waves
Beneath the bow, the thrust
Of powered oars, the manweight
Amidships. What we need:
Purpose.

Off the sea grass
Back at last
For once, one last time
Against the pitted sea.

Godspeed

Shearing off
From the rock-rimmed reach
The lithe craft
Lifts her pointed snout
Drops to the wave trough
Repeats, and again repeats.

We are off Turtle Neck heading north northeast
With a steady breeze
And clear skies.

The boat does most of the work.
We angle the sails,
Mind the wheel,
And find that there is time for talk.

The trip is context
And the conversation from the heart
Not constrained by time or secret motive
Dynamic even in its pauses
The inconsequential at ease
With the profound
Values articulated in the rough
Intimate things touched on
Decisions brought up
And decided
Or put away for another day

No matter. All that's needed
Is the benediction
Of each others' trust.

Godspeed works through the choppy seas;
So do we. And seek safe harbor
As the sun flattens toward the horizon
And the new moon
Cups gentle darkness in the west.

Intervals

It's a little compulsive, I admit.
I count time, intervals, cycles
So many ways it's like a picture
Of gears within gears beside
Other gears within gears
All ratcheting away
At obscure velocities
Unrelated, one to another.

And I don't mean just common things
Like birthdays and anniversaries,
No, I know how long my tube of toothpaste lasts,
When I emptied the wastebasket
When I started this bar of soap
When I put the toilet paper
On its springy roller thing.

(I told you it was compulsive.)

And there's a lot more: odometers
And haircuts, lawn mowings,
And oil changes, all tabulated,
All in neat mental folders.

But there is one clock
Above all clocks
Whose shining face
Measures out my life,
My reverence.

It's the moon.
Wherever I am
Day or night

I can tell you
(About) where the moon is;
And however many times
I see the moon
I hunger to see it yet again.

Some years ago
Shortly after dark
I was walking a path
Among walnut, hickory and oak
And watching the full moon
Rise in a golden crescendo
Between the black trees
Hushed with nightfall.

I idly computed the number
Of full moon risings left for me
To watch before I die
(More compulsion, I confess).

The number was about five hundred.
"That's not enough,"
I said aloud, with a sharp note of fear.

I checked my math.
It was correct.
"Not nearly enough," I muttered.

Since then the kids have finished growing.
The dog died.
The new dog went from pup to patriarch.

Bars of soap and tubes of toothpaste
March across my mental spreadsheet
In disheartening profusion.

And you know what?
Since that lovely night
I've never updated my full moon count.
Can't do it.

There's a core of fear
About the number,
About how few full moons
There are left for me to savor
Before they go on without me.

Degrees Of Silence

Walking near dark
In an early November snowfall
In a field edged by woods impenetrable

A big field, and separated
From another just as big
Only by the thinnest strip
Of trees and bracken

Here a man can walk for hours
In the new, wet snow
Huge flakes cartwheeling down
To become tears on my cheek
Or blossoms in my hair

I walk the edge of field and wood
Watching grasses topped with a ridge of snow
Arching down delicately
And tree limbs with the same load
But unbowed

The light going out by degrees
The snowfall muting sound
And my deliberate progress
Becomes a thing not of necessity only
But certitude, and finally joy itself.

Easter Walk

Wind and rain
A tumult of ragged clouds

Such turbulence
Is a kind of harmony.

I walk
On a small path
In a large wilderness

Pelted down
A sodden sliver

Not seeking meaning
But open to it.

I've never known
What I was looking for,
Only that I was looking.

I may have found it
Without realization.

I think
Perhaps
Every raindrop
Is God's whisper.

Made in the USA
Charleston, SC
01 February 2015